LIVES
AND
TIMES

Beatrix Potter

Jayne Woodhouse

Heinemann Interactive Library
Des Plaines, Illinois

Designed by Ken Vail Graphic Design, Cambridge, England
Illustrations by Alice Englander
Printed in Hong Kong / China

03 2 01 00 99
10 9 8 7 6 5 4 3 2 1

Library of Congress Cataloging-in-Publication Data
Woodhouse, Jane, 1952-
    Beatrix Potter / Jayne Woodhouse.
       p.   cm. — (Lives and times)
    Includes bibliographical references and index.
    Summary: An introductory biography of the author and artists of
many books for children, including the favorite "Tale of Peter Rabbit."
    ISBN 1-57572-667-X (lib. bdg.)
    1. Potter, Beatrix, 1866-1943—Biography—Juvenile literature.
    2. Authors. English—20th century—Biography—Juvenile literature.
    3. Artists—Great Britain—Biography—Juvenile literature.
    4. Children's stories—Authorship—Juvenile literature.
    [1. Potter, Beatrix, 1866-1943. 2. Authors, English. 3. Artists.
    4. Women—Biography.] I. Title. II. Series: Lives and times (Des Plaines, Ill.)
    PR6031.072797   1998
    823'.912
    [B]--DC21   97-50364
                                                                  CIP
                                                                  AC

Acknowledgments
The Publishers would like to thank the following for permission to reproduce photographs:
Michael Dyer Association Ltd. p. 16; National Trust Photographic Library: pp. 20, 21; F. Warne & Co.:
pp. 17, 21, 22, 23, Courtesy of Victoria and Albert Museum pp. 18, 19.

Cover photograph reproduced with permission of The Victoria & Albert Museum and F. Warne & Co.

Our thanks to Betty Root for her comments in the preparation of this book.

Every effort has been made to contact copyright holders of any material reproduced in this book.
Any omissions will be rectified in subsequent printings if notice is given to the Publisher.

Some words are shown in bold, **like this**. You can find out what they mean
by looking in the glossary.

Contents

Part One

Have you heard of Peter Rabbit, Jemima Puddle-Duck, or Squirrel Nutkin? You will find them all in little books written by the same **author**. Her name is Beatrix Potter.

Beatrix Potter was born in London, England, in 1866. As a girl, Beatrix and her family lived in a big house and had **servants** to look after them.

Beatrix was a very lonely girl. She wasn't allowed to have any friends and she didn't go to school. A **governess** taught Beatrix at home.

Beatrix's only friends were her pets. She had pet mice, snails, bats, hedgehogs, frogs, lizards, and a rabbit named Peter.

Beatrix loved to draw and paint. She spent hours watching her animals and drawing them. Her pictures were very good.

When Beatrix grew up, she had to stay at home to look after her parents. She was often bored and sad. Her happiest times were her trips to the country or the time she spent painting.

When Beatrix was 27 years old, she wrote a special letter to a little boy who was ill. In the letter was a story about a rabbit named Peter. The story had many of Beatrix's pictures.

Beatrix thought that maybe other children would like to read her story. She made the letter into a book and drew a picture for each page. She called it *The Tale of Peter Rabbit.*

Beatrix sent the book to six **publishers.**
They didn't like it and sent it back. Finally,
a man named Frederick Warne said he
would publish it.

Children loved *Peter Rabbit*. Mr. Warne asked Beatrix to write more books. Beatrix had found a way of using her painting skills and her love of animals.

Beatrix always loved the countryside. So she bought a farm. She called the farm Hill Top. When she was 47, she married William Heelis, a man who lived near Hill Top.

Soon Beatrix stopped writing books. She
began to buy and look after more farms.
People forgot that Mrs. Heelis was once
Beatrix Potter, the famous **author.** She
died in 1943, when she was 77 years old.

Part Two

It is almost 100 years since Beatrix Potter wrote *The Tale of Peter Rabbit* and other books. Children today still love her stories. They are printed in many languages and in **braille**.

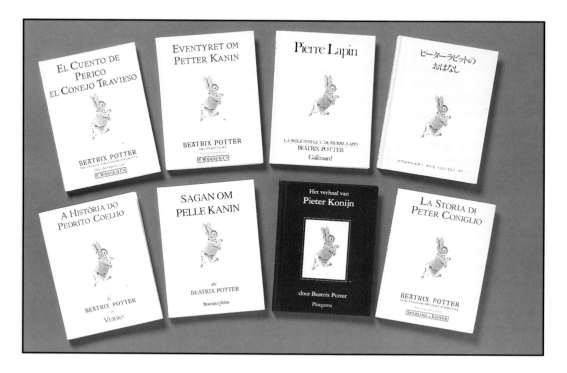

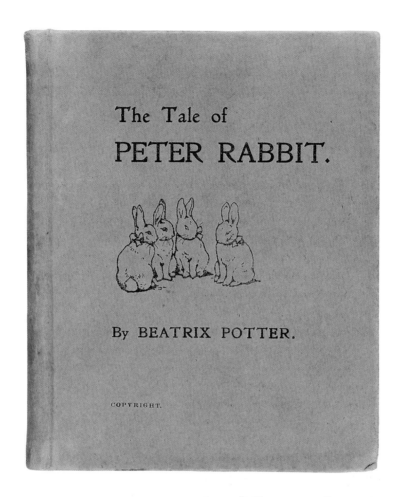

Beatrix was once asked how she made up such enjoyable stories. "I have just made stories to please myself," she said, "because I never grew up."

Photographs of Beatrix Potter show us what she looked like at different times in her life.

Beatrix's house, Hill Top, is now a **museum**. Inside you can see how she lived. Her furniture, pictures, and clothes are still there.

Beatrix wrote some of her books at Hill Top. You can see parts of the farmhouse in the pictures in her books.

This is a page from Beatrix's secret **diary**. It is written in **code**. The code was figured out a long time after she died. This special diary tells us many things about her life.

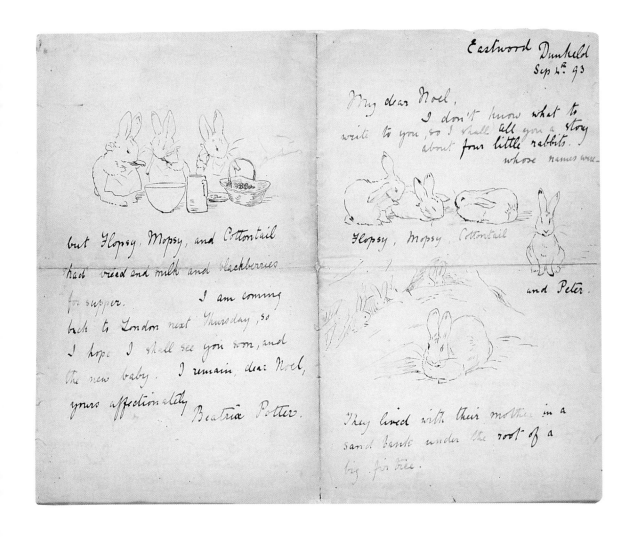

Beatrix's picture letter about Peter Rabbit is still around. Can you read the beginning of the story?

Glossary

author person who writes books

braille special kind of writing for blind people in which they feel raised dots on paper with their fingertips

code set of letters, words, or symbols that has a secret meaning

diary book in which a person writes about what happens in his or her life everyday

governess woman who teaches children at their home

museum building that has objects that tell us about science, art, history, or a special person

publishers people who make books

servants people who work in the homes of other people

Index

More Books to Read

Carr, Sally G., and Bronwen Hall. *The Story of Beatrix Potter.* Baltimore: Calvert School, 1995.

Johnson, Jane. *My Dear Noel: The Story of a Letter from Beatrix Potter.* New York: Dial Books, 1998.

Wallner, Alexandra. *Beatrix Potter.* New York: Holiday House, 1995.